JOSIAH BALOS

55 Things To See In Tennessee
Travel Guide for Kids and Their Parents

Copyright © 2023 by Josiah Balos

All rights reserved. No part of this publication may be reproduced, stored or transmitted in any form or by any means, electronic, mechanical, photocopying, recording, scanning, or otherwise without written permission from the publisher. It is illegal to copy this book, post it to a website, or distribute it by any other means without permission.

Josiah Balos asserts the moral right to be identified as the author of this work.

Josiah Balos has no responsibility for the persistence or accuracy of URLs for external or third-party Internet Websites referred to in this publication and does not guarantee that any content on such Websites is, or will remain, accurate or appropriate.

Designations used by companies to distinguish their products are often claimed as trademarks. All brand names and product names used in this book and on its cover are trade names, service marks, trademarks and registered trademarks of their respective owners. The publishers and the book are not associated with any product or vendor mentioned in this book. None of the companies referenced within the book have endorsed the book.

First edition

*This book was professionally typeset on Reedsy.
Find out more at reedsy.com*

Contents

1	Introduction	1
2	Music City Fun Facts	3
3	55 Things to See in Tennessee	5
4	Indoor and Outdoor Play	13
5	Music City's Seasonal Showcase	17
6	Country Music Magic	25
7	Tasty Food in Nashville	29
8	Nashville's Neighborhoods Unveiled	37
9	Music City on Every Budget	45
10	The Ultimate Family Adventure	51
11	Bonus Itinerary	53
About the Author		57

1

Introduction

Hey there! Welcome to Nashville! It's a place where awesome country music mixes with the yummy smells of Southern food, and everyone is super friendly. This is your "Travel Guide for kids and their parents: Nashville, TN; 55 Things To See In Tennessee."

Imagine you're standing at a big crossroad, trying to figure out where to go on your next family adventure. You want to have loads of fun, make exciting memories, and have the best time ever! But there are so many choices, it's like, "Where do we even start?" Well, that's where this guide comes in, and I'm so excited to be your guide buddy.

I'm not your regular guidebook writer; I'm 10 years old and I live right here in Nashville, I'm Josiah. My family and I have checked out all the cool adventures in and around town. We've explored all the famous places and the hidden treasures. I'm like your local expert, and I want to share all the amazing things you can do in Nashville with your family.

This guide is like a special key to open up all the fun in Music City, which is what everyone calls Nashville. You can dive into the heart of country music, taste the super spicy hot chicken, run around in beautiful parks, and have awesome adventures with your family. We've got all kinds of stuff, from things that don't cost much to things that'll make you feel like a millionaire.

When you flip through the pages of this guide, you won't just find the famous places tourists go to. You'll also discover cool parks and playgrounds where you and your friends and family can have a blast. There are hiking trails that take you to incredible views, restaurants that love having families over, fun events happening at different times of the year, and a bunch more.

Whether you're a huge music fan, a foodie who loves to eat, or just a family looking for a super fun vacation, there's something here for you. So, grab this guide, bring your sense of adventure, and let's get ready for an awesome journey. I'll guide you through everything, making sure your visit to Nashville is like a happy song and a super cool adventure you'll always remember.

Now, let's start our journey together with the first chapter, where we'll explore the heart of Nashville, the city's famous music scene, and why it's the best place for your family to visit. Yeehaw!

2

Music City Fun Facts

I love learning about the history of a city when I visit and all the things that make that city unique. Here are some of my favorite fun facts about Nashville, Tennessee. You can go back home and show off to all your friends and family about all the things you discovered on your adventure to Nashville.

"Music City," is its super awesome secret name! It's because this place is like the king of all music. People all over the world know about it. You see, in Nashville, there are more songs, guitars, and singers than anywhere else. It's where all the big music stars make their songs, like country music heroes and even famous rock and pop bands. So, they call it "Music City" because it's where all the coolest tunes are born, and it's a place where music magic happens every day!

Oh, you won't believe the story of Nashville's famous hot chicken! It's a spicy adventure that started a very, long time ago. There was this guy named Prince Thornton, and he loved fried chicken. One day, his girlfriend got really mad at him, and to get back at him, she made his chicken super duper spicy with a fiery blend of spices. But guess what?

Instead of getting all upset, he loved it! It was so good that he shared it with his friends and family. And that's how hot chicken became a Nashville legend. Now, you can find hot chicken in lots of places all over Nashville, and people from everywhere come to taste that delicious, spicy chicken. It's like a tasty tale of love, revenge, and a mouthful of flavor!

There is also this building called the Parthenon in Nashville, and it looks exactly like the original one in Greece! A long time ago, in 1897, Nashville hosted a big fair called the Tennessee Centennial Exposition to celebrate 100 years of Tennessee. They decided to build a full-size copy of the ancient Parthenon from Greece right in the park. It's like having a piece of ancient history in our city! They made it with big columns and everything, just like in the old days. Inside, there's a giant statue of a lady named Athena. People come from all over to see it and pretend they're back in ancient Greece. It's like a time machine that takes you back in time without leaving Nashville!

The people in Nashville are the friendliest folks you'll ever meet! It's like a big, warm hug from everyone you see. When you walk down the street, they say "hi y'all" like they've known you forever. If you need directions or have questions, they're always there to help. And the best part is when they talk, you can hear that sweet Southern accent that makes you feel right at home. They're so welcoming, it's like having a whole city full of new friends, and that's what makes Nashville even more amazing!

3

55 Things to See in Tennessee

Alrighty, let's dive into the fun in Nashville, Tennessee! This chapter is like a treasure map to the top 55 best things to do in Music City, and it's gonna be a blast. We've got the big famous spots and the awesome local secrets, all perfect for families like yours. And guess what? I'm gonna tell you about them in great detail, so you can imagine what it's really like. Plus, I've split them into "Main Attractions" and "Local Favorites," so you can pick the ones that sound the most ideal for your family. It's gonna be a wild adventure!

Main Attractions:

1. **The Grand Ole Opry:** It's a huge concert spot where people sing country songs! You can stomp your feet and clap your hands to the music.
2. **Country Music Hall of Fame and Museum:** It's a big museum filled with guitars, shiny costumes, and even hats from famous country singers. You can pretend to be a country star!
3. **Ryman Auditorium:** This place is a magical stage where famous people in cowboy boots once sang. You can stand where they stood

and maybe even sing your own song.
4. **Nashville Zoo:** The zoo is like a real-life animal adventure! You can see lions, tigers, and even play with goats and sheep in a special area.
5. **Adventure Science Center:** It's a playground for your brain! You can touch cool science stuff and even see stars in a big round room.
6. **Cheekwood Estate and Gardens:** Imagine a secret garden with pretty flowers, statues, and fountains. It feels like you're in a fairy tale.
7. **Belle Meade Plantation:** This place is literally frozen in time! You can learn about people who lived a long time ago and explore their big house.
8. **Parthenon in Centennial Park:** It's a giant castle made of stone. Inside, there's a super big statue and a cool art museum.
9. **Nashville Shores Lakeside Resort:** It's a giant water park near a lake! You can go down water slides, play in the sand, and swim in the lake.
10. **Tennessee State Museum:** This museum is like a treasure chest full of old stuff! You can see swords, clothes, and even a big boat.
11. **Frist Art Museum:** It's a place with really cool pictures and sculptures. You can look at them and maybe even try to make your own art!
12. **Andrew Jackson's Hermitage:** You'll get to step back in time and see how people used to live. You can explore a big house and pretty gardens.
13. **Lane Motor Museum:** It's a place with lots of cars! Some look really strange, like they're from the future. You can pretend to drive them.
14. **Bicentennial Capitol Mall State Park:** It's a large park with a map of Tennessee in the ground. You can run around, have a picnic, and learn about the state. Very close to this park is one of

our favorite playgrounds: Frankie Pierce Park.
15. **Belmont Mansion:** This place is a castle in the city. You can explore the fancy rooms and imagine being a prince or princess.
16. **Johnny Cash Museum:** It's all about a famous singer! You can see his shiny outfits, guitars, and even hear his songs.
17. **Nashville Children's Theatre:** It's where people put on plays and act out stories. You can watch them act, it's like watching a real-life storybook.
18. **Tennessee Agricultural Museum:** this place is a farm in a building! You can see tractors, animals, and things farmers use.
19. **Adventureworks Zipline Tours:** It's a super fun adventure where you zip through the treetops. It's like being a bird for a little bit!
20. **Tennessee State Capitol:** This place sits atop a big hill so it looks really majestic and it's the place where people in charge make rules. You can see where they sit and talk about the state.
21. **Nashville Public Library:** It's a giant library with a beautiful outdoor courtyard and a fun kids section with a climbing bring inside! They have amazing puppet shows there; so check if one is happening when you're in town. You can read awesome stories, hear new ones, and also play games.
22. **Radnor Lake State Park:** It's like a magical forest with a beautiful lake. You can hike, see animals, and enjoy the quiet nature.
23. **Historic RCA Studio B:** It's where famous singers recorded their songs! You can see old microphones and imagine singing like a star.
24. **The Escape Game:** You can solve puzzles and riddles to escape from different rooms. It's like being a detective or an explorer!
25. **Musicians Hall of Fame and Museum:** It's like a hall of heroes for music! You can learn about amazing musicians and see their instruments.
26. **Edwin and Percy Warner Parks**: These are very big parks with

trails and trees. You can hike, have picnics, play in creeks and even see deer!

27. **Belle Meade Winery:** It's where grown-ups taste yummy grape juice while looking at grape vines. You can pretend to be a little winemaker.
28. **Tennessee Central Railway Museum:** It's a place with old trains! You can hop on a real train and learn how they chug-chug.
29. **Historic Travelers Rest Plantation and Museum:** This place is like going back to a time when people wore funny clothes. You can learn about history and explore a big garden.
30. **Stones River National Battlefield:** It's where soldiers had big battles a long time ago. You can learn about history and see where the fighting happened.
31. **Nashville Armory:** It's where you can learn about guns and how to use them safely. It's like being in a video game, but it's real.
32. **Nissan Stadium:** It's where big football games happen! You can watch the teams play, cheer, and have lots of fun.

Local Favorites:

1. **Cumberland Park:** It's a super cool playground by the river! There are slides, fountains to splash in, and places to climb. You can have a picnic with your family and play all day. It's got the best view of the city.
2. **Fort Negley Park:** This place is like an ancient fort with big walls. You can climb up high and see the whole city. It's an awesome spot for exploring and learning about history.
3. **Percy Priest Lake:** It's a giant lake where you can go swimming and boating. You can have a fun day in the water with your family!
4. **Fort Nashborough:** It's a pretend fort like the ones from a long time ago. You can play like you're defending the fort from pretend

bad guys and imagine you're a brave hero.
5. **Shelby Bottoms Nature Center:** It's a nature wonderland with trails and animals. You can hike and learn about plants and critters, like birds and frogs. Our favorite things to do in this park are playing at the dirt park by the Nature Center and discovering the Hidden Pond (there are usually lots of turtles). And if you love deer, the park is full of them – you can most often sight them in the early mornings or at night as the sun is setting. I wouldn't be surprised if you'd bump into me on your visit to this park – I ride my bike there pretty much every day of the year.
6. **Smith Springs Recreation Area:** It's by the water and has sandy beaches, so you can build sandcastles and swim. You can have a beach day right in Nashville!
7. **Fannie Mae Dees Park ("Dragon Park"):** This park is like a fairytale come true! There's a giant dragon to play on and cool play areas. It's a magical place for kids to use their imaginations. Parking is limited but when we go we usually find street parking.
8. **Cumberland River Pedestrian Bridge:** Imagine a super long bridge that goes over the river. You can walk or ride your bike and see the city from way up high. You can get on the bridge from Broadway Street or near the Nissan Stadium. Sometimes you can find parking on the small streets near the Nissan Stadium instead of the busy and pricey options off Broadway.
9. **Adventure Park at Nashville:** It's like an obstacle course in the trees! You can climb, swing, and zip through the forest like Tarzan or a ninja. It's an outdoor challenge for kids who love adventure. When I go with my friends, we have an absolute blast here. It has different skill levels so it could be fun for every age.There are also picnic tables so bring snacks or a picnic lunch.
10. **Shelby Park and Bottoms:** It's a big park with trails, so you can ride your bike or hike. You can even have a picnic by the river and

explore nature all around. I live right outside of the park!
11. **Stones River Greenway:** It's a trail by a river where you can bike or walk. You can see ducks and fish in the water, and it's perfect for nature-loving families.
12. **Fort Granger Park:** It's like a peaceful fort in a big park. You can have a picnic, play on the grass, and enjoy the nice outdoors.
13. **Nashville Greenway System:** It's like a web of trails all over the city. You can explore different parks and neighborhoods, riding your bike or walking with your family.
14. **The Nashville Palace:** It's a place with live country music, and you can even dance! Kids can stomp their feet and have fun listening to the tunes.
15. **Stones River Greenway:** It's a river trail where you can go on an adventure. You might see ducks and even deer if you're really lucky!
16. **Cumberland River Pedestrian Bridge:** You can walk on this super tall bridge and look at the river below. It's a great spot to watch boats and feel like you're on top of the world!
17. **Lane 5 Woodworks:** If you're into super-duper woodworking, Lane 5 is like a secret treasure chest. They make awesome custom wood furniture, and it's a place where you can see some of the coolest wood creations ever!
18. **Hatch Show Print:** This place has been making super cool posters for musicians since the 19th century. It's like going back to a time when posters were made by hand. You can even join in on a tour and make your own special poster.
19. **The Gallery of Iconic Guitars (GIG):** This super cool museum is at Belmont University. They've got a bunch of amazing old guitars that famous musicians used to rock out with. If you love music and guitars, you gotta check it out. Belmont University has a beautiful campus that's nice to walk around.

20. **The Mystery Mansion:** It's not a spooky place, don't worry! This is like a fun puzzle house where you have to solve clues to escape. It's like being in a real-life mystery.
21. **The Nashville Palace:** It's a country music spot that's not as crowded as the big famous ones. They have live shows and even a dance floor where you can practice your two-stepping!
22. **Franklin on Foot:** Take a tour in historic Franklin, Tennessee, with a guide who knows all the stories and secrets of the town. You'll hear about Civil War history, ghost stories, and more.
23. **Splash Pads:** Since it's so hot in Nashville through most of the summer having somewhere to splash around is key. Here are the Splash Pads in and near Nashville:

- **Cumberland Park Splash Pad (Nashville):** This place is like a water wonderland in the city. There are fountains that shoot up from the ground, and you can run through them, getting all wet and giggly.
- **Fannie Mae Dees Park Splash Pad (Dragon Park - Nashville):** It's not just a cool dragon statue here, but they also have a splash pad where you can splash around and have a blast.
- **Watkins Park Splash Pad (Nashville):** It's like a secret oasis with water sprayers that pop up from the ground. You can wear your swimsuit and enjoy the splashy fun.
- **The Avenue Splash Pad (Murfreesboro):** This one's a bit outside Nashville, but it's worth it. They've got a splash pad and even a big bucket that dumps water. It's a super cool way to cool off on a hot day.
- **CoolSprings Galleria Splash Pad (Franklin, TN):** Franklin is just a short drive from Nashville. At this mall, they have a splash pad where you can run around and cool down after shopping.
- **Larry Keeton Theatre Splash Pad (Donelson, TN):** It's like a

hidden splash pad gem. You can splash and play in the water and have a blast with your friends.

- **Bellevue's Red Caboose Park Splash Pad (Nashville):** It's not just a train park; they have a splash pad where you can have wet and wild fun.

With this awesome list, you're absolutely ready to discover all the amazing stuff in Nashville, from the most famous places to the secret treasures that make this city extraordinary. Every single one is like a special memory waiting to happen for you and your family. So, let's kick off this adventure and jump right into the heart of Music City, where there are songs, stories, and magic all around!

4

Indoor and Outdoor Play

There are lots of awesome places to play in Nashville, some are inside, some are outside. Let me tell you all about them!

Indoor Play

Indoor play is great when it's too hot or rainy outside. One spot you could check out is the Adventure Science Center. You can discover science and even see stars inside a big round room. There are museums too, like the Country Music Hall of Fame, where you can see shiny guitars and learn about country music heroes. Opryland is a giant hotel with five huge indoor gardens. But watch out for SoundWaves; it's the best waterpark experience you will get; and it's classy too. You could also Bowl with your family if you want to knock down some pins.

Pros:

- **Stay Dry and Cool:** One of the best things about indoor activities is that you can have loads of fun, even if it's pouring rain outside or

super hot. No need to worry about getting wet or sweaty!
- **Lots of AC:** They usually have this thing called air conditioning, which is like having a magical breeze inside. So, you won't feel all sweaty and sticky while you play.
- **No Sunburn:** You won't get a sunburn inside, which means no need for icky sunscreen. Your skin stays safe and happy.
- **Year-Round Fun:** Indoor places are usually open all year, so you can have a blast in any season, whether it's summer, winter, or anything in between.
- **Awesome Adventures:** Indoor places often have cool adventures like science experiments, art, or water parks. You can have exciting experiences without worrying about the weather.

Cons:

- **Sometimes Crowded:** Because indoor places are so cool, lots of other people want to go there too. So, it can get a bit crowded, and you might have to wait in line for some things.
- **Not as Much Space:** Indoor places might not have as much space as the great outdoors. So, if you love running around and playing tag, you might have to be careful not to bump into things.
- **Entrance Fees:** Some indoor places might charge a fee to get in, so it's not always free. But the good news is, you often get a lot of fun for your money!

So, indoor activities are like a comfy, air-conditioned adventure, where you can have a blast without worrying about the weather. Just be ready for some fun and maybe a bit of waiting in line.

Outdoor Play

If you want to run around outside, there are lots of playgrounds and parks. Shelby Bottoms Nature Center is like a nature playground with trails and animals. You can go hiking and see wildlife. Some hikes even have waterfalls; that's like finding hidden treasure! There's a ropes course if you're up for an adventure in the trees. You can also go kayaking or canoeing on the water, ride horses, or watch sports. The Sounds Baseball team is like your home team. The Nashville Soccer Club is all about soccer, and you can cheer really loud for them. But don't forget the skilled Titans, and the smashing Predators.

Pros:

- **Fresh Air and Sunshine:** When you're playing outside, you get to breathe in the nice, fresh air, and feel the warm sunshine on your face. It's an awesome natural playground!
- **Lots of Space to Run:** Outdoors, you have tons of space to run around, play games, and have adventures. You can be as wild as you want!
- **Nature Exploration:** You can explore nature and see all sorts of cool things like birds, trees, and even bugs. It's like being on your very own nature show!
- **No Entrance Fees:** Most outdoor places like parks and playgrounds are usually free, so you can have fun without spending money.
- **Year-Round Fun:** Just like indoor places, you can have outdoor fun all year round. In summer, you can splash in the water, and in winter, you can build snowmen or have leaf fights in the fall.

Cons:

- **Weather Worries:** Sometimes, the weather doesn't cooperate. It can get super hot in the summer, or rainy and cold when you least expect it. That can be a bit of a bummer.
- **No AC:** Unlike indoor places, there's no air conditioning outdoors. So, if it's hot, you might feel all sweaty, and if it's chilly, you could get a bit cold.
- **Sunburn Alert:** When you're out in the sun, you need to be careful not to get a sunburn. So, you might have to wear sunscreen and a hat to protect your skin.
- **Critters and Bugs:** While exploring nature is super fun, you might meet some critters and bugs along the way. So, be ready to make some new tiny friends!
- **Limited Play Equipment:** Some outdoor activities might have limited play equipment, like swings or slides, so you might have to take turns with other kids. But taking turns can be fun, it's a chance to make new friends.

So, outdoor activities are like a big, open adventure with fresh air and space to run. Just keep an eye on the weather and make sure to stay safe from the sun and bugs!

5

Music City's Seasonal Showcase

Visiting Nashville throughout the year is like turning the pages of a never-ending storybook filled with adventures waiting for your family. Let's dive into the magic of each season!

Spring time in Nashville

When spring arrives in Nashville, it feels like the whole city comes to life! The weather is just perfect for being outdoors, and the flowers start blooming everywhere. One of the most magical places to visit during this season is Cheekwood Estate and Gardens. It's like stepping into a fairytale garden with a variety of pretty flowers. You can even pack a picnic and have a lovely lunch among the blossoms. But here's a little secret – the best part is the Nashville Cherry Blossom Festival! It's a celebration of these stunning cherry blossoms, just like the ones you see in Japan. The trees burst into beautiful pink and white flowers, and it's like a dream. You can also try yummy Japanese food, like sushi and mochi. But there's a small thing to watch out for - sometimes rain showers surprise you. So, grab an umbrella just in case, and get ready for a springtime adventure in Nashville!

Spring in Nashville is super fun because you can do lots outdoors! One thing to do is go to the Nashville Zoo. You get to see all kinds of animals, and they have a big playground too (it's probably one of the best in all of Nashville) . It's like a huge wooden fort. Plus, they sometimes have special events like animal shows; depending on the holiday season the whole zoo is decorated.

And guess what? You can also have a splashing good time at Nashville Shores Lakeside Resort. They've got big water slides and even a sandy beach for building sandcastles. You can also swim in the lake, and it's so much fun on a sunny day.

If you like hiking, there's Radnor Lake State Park. It's a nature wonder with walking trails where you can see unique birds and even turtles by the lake. And don't forget your bicycle because there are great bike paths too!

Spring is also baseball time! You can go cheer for the Nashville Sounds at the baseball games. The team is great, and you can have hot dogs and popcorn while watching the game. And, if you like soccer, you can shout for the Nashville Soccer Club. They play exciting matches that you and your family can enjoy together.

Spring in Nashville is all about outdoor adventures with animals, water, nature, and cheering for your favorite teams. It's a blast!

Summer Fun in Music City

Summer in Nashville is an amazing time for family adventures. The sun is shining, and the city is full of exciting things to do. What's on the menu for a fun summer trip to Music City?

Nashville summers can get pretty hot, but don't worry, we've got you covered. You can head over to SoundWaves, which is a giant waterpark right in the heart of the Opryland Resort. SoundWaves has thrilling water slides that twist and turn before you plunge into cool pools. It's got a nice combination of indoor and outdoor pools, a big wave pool with a huge screen playing music (since it is Music City). They even have a wave simulation where you can ride the waves like a pro surfer. You can also relax on a lazy river, you can literally float on a gentle stream. It's a summer paradise for the whole family.

Summer is the perfect time for a picnic, and Nashville has some awesome parks where you can spread out your blanket and enjoy a meal together. Centennial Park is one of those places with beautiful gardens, a big pond, and even a full-scale replica of the Parthenon, which is pretty amazing! You can have a picnic near the pond and feed the ducks while enjoying the sun.

You know what else makes summer in Nashville special? Outdoor concerts! There are some super exciting places where you can listen to live music under the stars. One of those places is Ascend Amphitheater, right by the river. They host awesome shows, and you can even dance and sing along with your family. It's a memory-maker for sure!

If you're an adventure-loving family, you can explore the great outdoors. Nashville has some fantastic parks like Percy Warner Park and Edwin

Warner Park. They have hiking trails and even biking paths where you can ride together as a family and discover the beauty of nature.

Enjoy a game of frisbee golf with your family. Shelby Park has a great frisbee golf course where you can try your hand at this fun sport. It's like a combination of frisbee and golf, and you get to explore the park while having a blast with your family. So, if you're up for a unique and active summer adventure, frisbee golf is the way to go.

Summertime is a great time to include indoor activities, especially on the really hot days, and it does get really hot. Some favorite options for indoor activities are the Adventure Science Center, the Museums, and Opryland Hotel gardens.

Summer in Nashville is all about water fun, picnics, outdoor concerts, and adventures in the great outdoors. Just remember to wear sunscreen, so you don't turn into a lobster! With your sunscreen on and your family by your side, you're ready for an incredible summer in Music City.

Fall Adventures in Nashville

Fall in Nashville is fantastic because the trees turn all kinds of colors, it can look like a magical storybook coming to life. The air gets a little cooler, and the trees all around the city start changing colors. It's the perfect time for family adventures! So, what can you do to make your fall unforgettable in Music City?

One of the best things about fall is the beautiful leaves changing colors. You can take a drive on the Natchez Trace Parkway, which is just outside of Nashville. The trees along this road turn into bright reds, oranges, and yellows, making it like a painting. You can enjoy all the changing colors, take pictures, and even have a picnic along the way.

Fall isn't complete without a trip to a pumpkin patch. Lucky for you, there are some fantastic pumpkin patches near Nashville. Shuckles Pumpkin Patch or Gentry's Farm are some of the coolest places where you can pick your own pumpkin, go on a hayride, and even get lost in a corn maze.

Speaking of corn mazes, there are a few around Nashville that are perfect for families. One of them is Lucky Ladd Farms. They have a gigantic corn maze with twists and turns to challenge your navigation skills. It's like a puzzle made out of corn!

Fall is the best time for hiking, and the trails around Nashville come alive with color. You can explore places like Cummins Falls State Park, which has beautiful trails leading to waterfalls. The best part is, you can dip your toes in the cool water and enjoy a family picnic by the falls.

Fall is all about cozy flavors, and that means pumpkin spice everything! You can visit local bakeries and cafes to savor pumpkin spice lattes, apple ciders, muffins, and pies. It's like tasting the season!

Nashville hosts some fantastic fall festivals. The Tennessee State Fair is a must-visit, where you can enjoy rides, games, and lots of yummy fair food. There's also the Celebrate Nashville Cultural Festival, where you can experience cultures from around the world. It's like taking a trip around the world all while still being in Nashville.

If you're in town around Halloween, you can explore the haunted history of Nashville. There are spooky ghost tours that take you to the most mysterious places in the city. It's a thrilling way to learn about the past and maybe even meet a friendly ghost!

Fall in Nashville is all about colorful leaves, pumpkin patches, corn mazes, hiking among waterfalls, cozy treats, festivals, and maybe even a spooky adventure. It's the perfect season for making family memories that will warm your heart on those cool autumn days.

Winter Magic in Music City

It's also the holiday season, and you must visit the Gaylord Opryland's "ICE!" exhibit, where they have amazing ice sculptures. Just remember, it can be cold, so bring your mittens and a warm coat.

Winter in Nashville is like a cozy blanket of fun and magic, and there are tons of cool things to do with your family. The air gets crisp, and the city transforms into a winter wonderland. So, what's on the list for a fantastic winter adventure in Music City?

One of the most magical things about winter is ice skating, and you can do it right in the heart of the city! The Ascend Amphitheater transforms into a twinkling ice skating rink, and it's perfect for families. You can glide on the ice, hold hands, and make some wobbly but fun memories. They even have hot chocolate to warm you up.

Nashville gets all dressed up in twinkling holiday lights. You can take a drive through the Dancing Lights of Christmas at Jellystone Park, where millions of lights dance to the beat of holiday music.

You know who's in Nashville during the winter? Santa Claus himself!

You can visit his house at the Santa's Wonderland in Bass Pro Shops. It's like stepping into the North Pole, and you can tell Santa what you'd like for Christmas.

Nashville loves Christmas parades, and they're a treat for the whole family. You can see fantastic floats, marching bands, and even Santa Claus shows up. It's a live holiday show right on the streets!

You can catch some super cool holiday shows in Nashville. The Nutcracker is a classic, and you can see the beautiful ballet. Or you can enjoy a holiday concert where they play all your favorite Christmas songs. It's a musical winter dream!

Winter can be chilly, so it's also a great time for indoor adventures. You can explore cool museums like the Frist Art Museum or the Adventure Science Center. They have hands-on exhibits, and it's a great way to learn and have fun.

You can't have winter without hot cocoa! Nashville has some amazing cafes and bakeries where you can warm up with a cup of hot chocolate topped with marshmallows and whipped cream. It's like a hug in a mug!

The year ends with a bang in Nashville. You can celebrate New Year's Eve with your family at the Jack Daniel's Music City Midnight. It's the biggest party with live music, fireworks, and the iconic Music Note Drop to welcome the new year.

Winter in Nashville is a time for ice skating, holiday lights, Santa visits, parades, shows, indoor adventures, hot cocoa, and ringing in the new year with a bang. It's a season of joy, warmth, and family fun in Music City!

Visiting Nashville in every season is like flipping through the pages of a vibrant, ever-changing storybook. Spring blooms with the colors of new beginnings, with cherry blossoms and picnics in the park. Summer sizzles with waterpark adventures, outdoor concerts, and endless sunshine. Fall paints the city with a warm, golden glow, as you explore pumpkin patches and corn mazes. Winter brings a magical wonderland of ice skating, holiday lights, and heartwarming festivities. No matter when you choose to visit, Nashville opens its doors to endless family adventures, ensuring that every season brings its own unique and unforgettable charm.

6

Country Music Magic

Nashville is like a giant music playground, and country music is the star of the show. It's like a cozy home for country musicians. When you walk down the streets, you can hear guitars strumming and people singing their hearts out. There are more guitars and cowboys here than you can count! It's a place where country music was born and where it lives and breathes every day.

Guess what? Some of the biggest country music stars live right here. It's like living in a music superstar neighborhood. You might even bump into one at the grocery store! They're the ones who write those amazing songs you sing along to. It's like a magic place where your favorite songs come to life.

If you want to learn about country music, there are lots of places to do that. The Country Music Hall of Fame is like a wonderland filled with instruments of all kinds, fabulous costumes the musicians wore on stage, and all the stories of the country music heroes. You can explore their amazing world and even try to write your own songs!

There's live music everywhere you go in Nashville. You can go to a place called the Grand Ole Opry, which is a famous country music concert that's been happening for a long, long time. It's where all the greatest country stars take the stage and put on amazing performances. Or you can go to places like Honky Tonk Highway where you can hear live music on every corner. And if you're lucky, you might even see a real country music show with fiddles and banjos!

Here is a list of the main spots to find live music:

- **The Grand Ole Opry:** The most famous place for country music shows. It's like the country music king's castle.
- **Broadway Honky Tonk Highway:** It's a street full of restaurants and honky-tonks where you can hear live music on every corner.
- **Bluebird Cafe:** A cozy little cafe where songwriters sing their songs and tell stories. It's super special!
- **Ryman Auditorium:** Known as the "Mother Church of Country Music," it's a historic and beautiful place for music shows.
- **The Station Inn:** If you love bluegrass music, this is the place to be. You can listen to pickin' and grinnin' all night.
- **Tootsie's Orchid Lounge:** A famous family friendly bar with a lot of history. You can enjoy live music and imagine all the legends who played there.
- **The Listening Room Cafe:** A great spot to hear songwriters perform their songs up close and personal.
- **3rd and Lindsley:** They have live music in a big, fun space, and you can even enjoy some yummy food.
- **The Bluegrass Inn:** As the name suggests, it's a wonderful place to enjoy bluegrass music and maybe even do a little dancing.
- **City Winery Nashville:** They combine great music with good

food and, of course, wine.
- **Acme Feed & Seed:** A fun multi-level spot where you can listen to live music and even do some dancing on the rooftop.

Nashville has these awesome places called honky-tonks where you can listen to live country music while having a root beer or some yummy food. It's like a party all day and night. And don't forget to check out the Bluebird Cafe, where you can see songwriters singing their songs and telling stories. It's like there is magic flowing through the air in this little cafe!

Here are the spots locals go for live music:

- **Douglas Corner Cafe:** This is a local favorite for songwriters and emerging musicians. It's a friendly spot to catch some live tunes.
- **The Family Wash/Garage Coffee:** A unique combination of a music venue and a coffee shop. It's a hidden gem for local music lovers.
- **The Five Spot:** A cool dive bar where you can catch live bands, including a variety of genres like rock, indie, and soul.
- **The End:** A legendary spot in the local music scene, known for hosting both up-and-coming and established bands.
- **The Basement:** A great place to discover indie and alternative music acts in a laid-back atmosphere.
- **Springwater Supper Club & Lounge:** One of Nashville's oldest dive bars, offering live music ranging from rock to punk.
- **Robert's Western World:** A classic honky-tonk with a local vibe, where you can enjoy live country music and even some dancing.

These local music hangouts are where you can experience the heart and soul of Nashville's music scene and discover some incredible local talent.

Nashville is like a country music amusement park where you can explore, learn, and listen to the most amazing music ever. It's where country music is more than just songs; it's a way of life!

7

Tasty Food in Nashville

Hey there, food adventurers! Nashville isn't just about twangy tunes and cowboy boots; it's also a foodie's dream come true. I'm here to take you on a mouthwatering journey through Music City's food scene. Whether you're into Southern comfort, smoky barbecue, fiery hot chicken, or just a classic cheeseburger, Nashville has a plate full of delights waiting for you.

We're going to explore the heartwarming world of Southern comfort food, where biscuits, fried chicken, and mac 'n' cheese are like an explosion for your taste buds. We'll dive into the sizzling world of barbecue, where ribs, pulled pork, and baked beans rule the menu. And you better be ready for some hot chicken, the spiciest journey you'll ever take!

But that's not all; we'll discover Nashville's beloved classics, family-friendly spots for young foodies, bakeries with the sweetest treats, and farmers' markets that are seriously food delights. Bring your appetite and let's explore the delicious side of Nashville together!

"Savoring Nashville's Southern Comfort"

Dive into the heartwarming world of Southern comfort food in Nashville. Let's explore the classic dishes that warm your soul, from buttery biscuits to crispy fried chicken and creamy mac 'n' cheese.

Top Restaurants:

- Loveless Cafe
- Puckett's Grocery & Restaurant
- Arnold's Country Kitchen
- Monell's Dining & Catering

"Nashville's Smoky Secrets"

Nashville's barbecue is legendary, let's go on a smoky adventure for your taste buds. Discover the best spots for mouthwatering ribs, pulled pork, and all the classic barbecue fixings.

Top Restaurants:

- Martin's Bar-B-Que Joint
- Edley's Bar-B-Que
- Peg Leg Porker
- Mission BBQ

"Hot Chicken Heat"

Get ready for some fiery fun with Nashville's famous hot chicken. Le'ts explore the history and culture of hot chicken and take you to the best places to experience the heat. If spicy is not your jam, they always have a mild option that's equally delicious.

Top Restaurants:

- Hattie B's Hot Chicken
- Prince's Hot Chicken
- Bolton's Spicy Chicken & Fish

"Nashville Classics"

Nashville has some beloved classics that you can't miss. From savory cheeseburgers to creamy milkshakes. Celebrate the timeless dishes that make Music City special by trying some of these restaurants.

Top Restaurants:

- Nashville's Pancake Pantry
- Rotier's Restaurant
- Sylvan Park Restaurant
- Jimmy Kelly's Steakhouse

"Family-Friendly Feasts in Music City"

Nashville is a family-friendly food destination, let's help you find restaurants where kids are not just welcome but excitedly catered to. Discover spots that offer delicious meals for the whole family.

Top Restaurants:

- The Pharmacy Burger Parlor & Beer Garden
- Burger Up

- Calypso Cafe
- Fido
- Biscuit Love
- Two Boots Pizza
- M.L. Rose Craft Beer & Burgers
- Marche Artisan Foods
- The Grilled Cheeserie

"Brews and Bakes"

Grown-ups can enjoy delicious brews at Nashville's breweries, while bakeries offer the sweetest treats in town. You'll uncover the best places for sips and sweets with these options.

Top Brews:

- Nashville's Yazoo Brewing Company
- TailGate Brewery
- Black Abbey Brewing Company
- Jackalope Brewing Company
- Little Harpeth Brewing
- Tennessee Brew Works

Top Bakes:

- The Cupcake Collection
- Baked on 8th
- Muddy's Bake Shop
- Proper Bagel (best bagels in town)

- Five Daughters Bakery
- Dozen Bakery
- Sunflower Bakehouse
- Sweet 16th Bakery
- Wild Muffin
- Frothy Monkey
- Stay Golden (my all time favorite)

Top Donuts:

- Five Daughters Bakery (best and most unique donuts – hands down)
- Fox's Donut Den
- Elliston Place Soda Shop
- Status Dough

"Farmers' Markets"

Nashville's farmers' markets are buzzing with local delicacies. Let me guide you to the markets where you can find fresh produce, artisanal goodies, and food trucks offering fresh and hot meals.

Markets:

- 12 South Farmers' Market
- East Nashville Farmers' Market
- Nashville Farmers' Market
- Richland Park Farmers' Market

"Food Trucks and Local Delights"

Explore Nashville's thriving food truck scene and discover the local delights that they serve. Take a culinary adventure through the streets of Music City by hunting down these food trucks and tasting their unique styles

Top Food Trucks:

- The Grilled Cheeserie
- Bad Luck Burger (best burger in Nashville)
- Biscuit Love
- Hattie B's Hot Chicken
- The Peach Cobbler Factory
- Smoke Et Al
- Deg Thai
- Yayo's OMG
- The Rolling Feast
- Music City Brisket

"Nashville's Sweet Tooth"

Got a sweet tooth? Nashville has you covered with its delectable desserts and treats. Let me introduce you to the best places for cupcakes, ice cream, and more.

Top Restaurants:

- The Goo Goo Shop & Dessert Bar

- GiGi's Cupcakes
- Yeast Nashville
- Jeni's Splendid Ice Cream
- Mike's Ice Cream
- Milk & Honey
- La Michoacana
- Buttermilk Sky Pie Shop
- Fryce Cream
- Tabla Rasa Toys (Soft Serve Ice Cream & awesome toy store connected to it – one of my favorites)

"International Cuisine in Nashville"

Nashville's got some amazing food from all over the world. Whether you want to try spicy Indian dishes, yummy Mexican tacos, or tasty Persian kebabs, this city's got it all. Let's dive into these delicious flavors together!

Top Restaurants:

- Woodlands Indian Cuisine (be sure to try the mango Lassi when you're there)
- Korea House
- Mangia Nashville
- Chauhan Ale & Masala House
- Rosepepper Cantina
- The Smiling Elephant
- Greko
- Germantown Cafe
- Butcher & Bee
- Casa Azafran

- Cafe Magot
- Adele's
- Zulema's Taqueria

From the finger-lickin' good hot chicken to the sweetest treats you can find, this city is a foodie's dream come true. And the best part? It's not just for grown-ups – there are tons of places that welcome families with open arms. So, whether you're chowing down on barbecue, exploring the local farmers' markets, or enjoying the yummy bakeries, Nashville's food scene is a delightful adventure waiting for you and your family. So grab your fork and get ready to taste the flavors of Music City.

8

Nashville's Neighborhoods Unveiled

Nashville has a bunch of different parts that are all super interesting. There's the East, South, West, North, and downtown - and they're all like their own little towns. In East Nashville, it's all about art and fun, while in South Nashville, you can find lots of history and music. West Nashville is where you go for trendy shops and yummy food, and North Nashville is all about being friendly and remembering the past. And downtown? Well, that's where all the bright lights and music happen! Each part has its own story to tell, and it makes Nashville a super cool place to explore!

East Nashville means Art

East Nashville is kind of like the super artsy heart of Music City! It's a place where art and family fun mix together perfectly. So, what's so special about East Nashville for families? Let's check it out!

First, there's this awesome place called Five Points in East Nashville. It's a super busy center with cool shops, yummy restaurants, and colorful street art. You can take a walk with your family and see all the murals or find cool souvenirs in the local shops.

And don't forget about Shelby Park! It's like a gigantic outdoor playground with a big green area. There's a playground for kids, walking trails to explore, and even a place for doggies to play. You can swing on the swings, dig in the dirt, or take a stroll by the Cumberland River.

Now, the food in East Nashville is seriously delicious! You can try some amazing southern comfort food at Edley's Bar-B-Que. Or if you're in the mood for tasty burgers, you've got Pharmacy Burger. Or try the local specialties at Marche Artisan Foods. Some of my personal favorites in East Nashville are Two Ten Jack, Butcher & Bee, Five Points Pizza & last but not least Grillshack Fries and Burgers.

Oh, and guess what? Music is everywhere in Nashville, including East Nashville. You can take your family to places like The 5 Spot or The Basement East. Another local favorite for outdoor live music is Friday's by the River in Shelby Park. These spots often have live music that's perfect for all ages.

And don't miss all the cool shops and boutiques in East Nashville. You can find unique stuff and souvenirs at places like The Frist Art Museum Gift Shop or Hey Rooster General Store or the Shoppes on Fatherland. Find amazing treasures to take home!

East Nashville also hosts family-friendly events all the time. For example, there's the Tomato Art Festival in August. It's a huge tomato party with art, music, and even a parade. You'll see tomatoes everywhere!

And finally, East Nashville is just bursting with creativity. You can visit art galleries like Red Arrow Gallery and see all kinds of colorful art. It's a big feast for your eyes!

East Nashville is kind of like a colorful and quirky neighborhood where family fun is waiting for you at every corner. Whether you're into art, delicious food, or awesome live music, East Nashville has a special charm that will make your family trip super unforgettable!

North Nashville Means History

North Nashville is the warm, friendly heart of Music City. It's where history, community, and good times come together for a perfect family adventure. So, why is North Nashville a unique and super cool place for families to visit? Let's find out!

One of the things that makes North Nashville unique is Fisk University. It's not just a regular university; it's famous for its incredible art collection, the Alfred Stieglitz Collection. You can take your family to see these amazing pieces of art, and maybe even get inspired to create your own masterpieces!

North Nashville is like a hub for history and culture. Buchanan Street is where you'll find lots of local businesses and artists. You can explore the cool art galleries and boutiques, and sometimes, there are fun community events and festivals too. It's like a little treasure trove of culture!

North Nashville is full of historic sites that can teach you about the past. You can visit the historic Jefferson Street, which was once a famous hub for African American music and culture. You'll step back in time to learn about the city's history.

North Nashville has some amazing places to eat. You can visit local favorites like Helen's Hot Chicken or Swett's Restaurant for delicious southern food. They're like hidden secret spots for foodies in the know!

Families Love Fannie Mae Dees Park, also known as "Dragon Park" because there's a giant dragon sculpture that you can climb on and explore.

North Nashville is a warm and welcoming neighborhood. The people here love their community, and you can often find local musicians playing live music in the streets. It can feel like your very own concert right on the sidewalk!

The Nashville Farmers' Market is a great place to visit. It's a big outdoor market where you can find fresh food, yummy snacks, and sometimes even special events. The park across from it is great for a walk, it even has a huge piano tune that plays on giant church bells on the hour.

North Nashville is full of culture, history, and delicious food. Whether you want to see art, learn about the past, or play at the Dragon Park, this neighborhood is full of surprises for families.

South Nashville Means Music

South Nashville is the heart of music. It's a place where you can explore rich culture, tasty food, and good times with your family. So, what makes South Nashville so unique and perfect for families to visit? Let me show you!

South Nashville is famous for its music, and the Country Music Hall of Fame is the kingdom of country music. You can take your family on a tour and learn all about the music legends. There are guitars, costumes, and even Elvis Presley's gold Cadillac!

The Ryman Auditorium is known as the "Mother Church of Country Music." It's where all the great musicians, like Johnny Cash and Dolly Parton, have performed. You can take a tour, and if you're lucky, you might even catch a live show.

South Nashville also has its unique history, you can explore Historic Printers Alley, which is full of stories from the past. You'll find cool restaurants, jazz clubs, and even hidden speakeasies. It's like taking a journey back in time!

South Nashville is the birthplace of hot chicken, and you can't visit without trying it! Places like Hattie B's or Prince's Hot Chicken are like spicy chicken heaven. Be ready for some heat, but it's oh-so-tasty!

If you have curious young minds in your family, the Adventure Science Center is a must-visit. Like a playground for your brain with interactive exhibits, cool planetarium shows, and even laser tag. It's super fun and educational at the same time!

South Nashville has some great parks. You can go to Sevier Park (Tuesday afternoons – May-Oct – are a great time to go since the 12 South Farmers Market happens), or visit Radnor Lake State Park for a nature adventure. It's like exploring the great outdoors right in the city! 12 South Street is a favorite tourist spot, lots of good food and shops to enjoy.

South Nashville is packed with history. You can visit the Tennessee State Capitol or Fort Negley, where you can learn about the Civil War. It will be a history lesson you'll actually enjoy!

Music is the heartbeat of South Nashville. You can often find live music in bars, restaurants, and even on the streets. So, keep your ears open for a catchy tune!

South Nashville is full of restaurants that welcome families. Places like The Pfunky Griddle or Arnold's Country Kitchen serve up delicious food and have a cozy atmosphere. It's like having a meal at a friend's house!

South Nashville is like a melody of music, history, and mouthwatering food. Whether you're exploring the music scene, learning about the past, or munching on hot chicken, this neighborhood is full of exciting adventures for families.

West Nashville Means Beauty

West Nashville is like the cool, trendy side of Music City. It's a place where you can discover awesome food, charming boutiques, and outdoor fun with your family. So, what's so unique about West Nashville, and why should families visit? Let's dive in and find out!

West Nashville is home to Cheekwood, a beautiful estate with colorful gardens. You can take your family on a stroll through these amazing gardens and enjoy the art sculptures.

Belle Meade Plantation is a historic mansion that feels like you stepped into a time machine and gone to the past. You can explore the old mansion, walk around the lovely grounds, and even meet some horses.

West Nashville is known for its foodie scene. You can taste some delicious dishes at places like The Loveless Café, where they serve amazing Southern comfort food and their famous biscuits.

The Belmont Mansion is like a fancy castle right in the city. You can tour the grand rooms, gardens, and even some hidden passageways.

Edwin and Percy Warner Parks are like your own slice of nature paradise in West Nashville. You can go hiking, have a family picnic, and even explore some trails. It's like having a big adventure right in the woods!

West Nashville is full of cool shops and boutiques. You can pick up unique gifts and treats at places like Pangaea and White's Mercantile.

Even in West Nashville, you can find live music. Spots like The Nashville Palace often have family-friendly shows.

There are many lovely parks in West Nashville, like McCabe Park or Charlotte Park. They're perfect for family playtime, whether it's swinging on the swings, playing ball, or having a picnic.

West Nashville has its fair share of cool breweries and bakeries. Places like TailGate Brewery and Dozen Bakery are great for family visits. It's a journey of taste and treats!

West Nashville is like a blend of beautiful gardens, delicious food, and nature adventures. Whether you're exploring historic mansions, discovering local shopping, or munching on yummy biscuits, this neighborhood is full of exciting family activities. It's a cozy and cool corner in Music City!

Nashville's neighborhoods are like colorful puzzle pieces that fit together to create a beautiful picture. Each one has its own special charm and adventures for families to enjoy. Whether you're exploring the music history of South Nashville, having a fairy tale day in West Nashville, or discovering the art and culture of East Nashville, there's something for everyone. It's like a big treasure map, and you and your family are the explorers. So, put on your adventure hats, grab your sense of wonder, and get ready to discover all the magic and excitement that Nashville's neighborhoods have to offer!

9

Music City on Every Budget

You can have fun in Nashville no matter how much money you have. Whether you're looking to have a great time without spending a dime or you want to splurge a little, Music City has something special for everyone. Let's get ready to discover the exciting adventures you can have in Nashville, no matter what's in your piggy bank!

Nashville on a Shoestring Budget

Hey there, budget-savvy explorers! Did you know you can have a blast in Nashville without spending a ton of cash? It's like a treasure hunt for fun, and here's how you can do it on a low budget or even for free!

- **Centennial Park:** Imagine a park with a big, shiny, full-sized replica of the Parthenon. That's Centennial Park! You can have a family picnic, roll down the grassy hills, or visit the free art gallery. It's like a mini Greek adventure right in Music City!
- **Shelby Bottoms Nature Center:** This place is like a nature

wonderland. You can explore the trails, spot wildlife, and even have a family day by the river. It's perfect for a low-budget outdoor adventure.
- **Musicians Corner:** It's like a free concert in the park! During the warmer months, you can enjoy live music at Centennial Park. Grab a blanket, some snacks, and let the music serenade you.
- **John Seigenthaler Pedestrian Bridge:** This bridge is like a scenic walkway with amazing views of downtown Nashville. It's perfect for a family stroll or to snap some cool photos.
- **Nashville Public Library:** Libraries are like treasure troves for bookworms and curious minds. You can check out books, enjoy storytime with your little ones, or even attend free events.
- **Street Art Hunting:** Nashville is like a big canvas. Explore different neighborhoods like East Nashville and The Gulch to find colorful street art and murals. It's like an art gallery on the streets! People line up to take pictures with the murals all over town, see how many you can find when you're visiting.
- **Live Music:** Believe it or not, you can find free live music in Music City. Some bars and venues offer free shows or open mic nights.
- **Honky Tonk Highway:** Broadway is like a neon-lit street filled with live music. You don't have to spend money on drinks; you can just enjoy the music and the lively atmosphere. It's like being part of a big, musical party!

So, you see, Nashville is full of free and low-budget adventures. It's like a playground for your wallet! Whether you're exploring parks, enjoying live music, or hunting for street art, you can have a fantastic time without breaking the bank. It's all about having fun the thrifty way.

Nashville's Thrifty Treasures

Hey, explorers with a little more jingle in your pockets! Nashville has plenty of exciting adventures for those with a medium budget. Let's dive into what you can do!

- **Adventure Science Center:** You can explore interactive exhibits, see cool planetarium shows, and even have hands-on science fun. It's like an adventure into outer space, right here on Earth!
- **Tennessee State Museum:** History buffs, this one's for you! You can visit the Tennessee State Museum and explore the state's past. It's like taking a journey through time and learning amazing stories.
- **Historic RCA Studio B:** Ever wondered where some of the most famous songs were recorded? Studio B is like a music time machine. You can take a tour and even record your own music. It's like stepping into a rock 'n' roll dream!
- **Frist Art Museum:** If you love art, you'll adore the Frist. It's like an art wonderland with changing exhibits, interactive art spaces, and even a café. It's a perfect place to explore your creative side.
- **The Escape Game:** Get ready for a thrilling adventure! The Escape Game is like a real-life puzzle you have to solve. You and your family can work together to find clues and unlock the mystery. It's like being in your very own detective story!
- **Musicians Hall of Fame and Museum:** For music-loving families, this place is packed with tunes. You can explore cool exhibits, see iconic instruments, and learn about legendary musicians. It's like a backstage pass to music history.
- **Foodie Delights:** In Nashville, you can enjoy some amazing meals without breaking the bank. Places like Biscuit Love and Hattie B's Hot Chicken offer delicious food with a side of local flavor. It's like a taste tour through Music City!

- Nashville is a fantastic place for medium-budget adventures. Whether you're diving into science, exploring history, creating your own music, or solving puzzles, there's something for everyone. It's like a world of fun waiting for you to explore!

Nashville's High-Flying Adventures

Hey, there, if money ain't a thing, what would you do in Nashville? Nashville is a place where luxury and top-tier experiences come to play. If you're looking to elevate your family's adventure with a high budget, you're in for a treat. Nashville rolls out the red carpet for you, offering a dazzling array of premium perks.

- **The Grand Ole Opry:** This place is like the crown jewel of country music. You can enjoy a show in style, complete with backstage tours and even a backstage dinner. It's like being a VIP in the world of country tunes! For a full experience of Opry, stay the night at the hotel and enjoy a day or two at the Soundwaves water park.
- **Ryman Auditorium:** The Ryman is like a music history book come to life. You can enjoy a backstage tour and get a peek at the stage that legends have graced.
- **Cheekwood Estate and Gardens:** If you love nature and art, this place is like a dream come true. You can stroll through beautiful gardens, explore art exhibits, and have a fancy afternoon tea.
- **Fine Dining:** Nashville's food scene is vibrant. With a high budget, you can savor meals at fine dining restaurants like The Catbird Seat and Husk.
- **Luxury Hotels:** Imagine staying in posh hotels like The Hermitage Hotel or the Omni Nashville. It's like having your own cozy castle

in Music City. You can enjoy pampering and top-notch service.
- **Live Music in Style**: In Nashville, you can enjoy live music in high style. Places like the Bluebird Cafe offer intimate concerts and premium experiences. You can have a private show with top-notch musicians.
- **Adventureworks Zipline Tours**: For thrill-seekers, this adventure is a high-flying dream. You can soar through the treetops on ziplines, enjoy beautiful nature, and even have a nighttime ziplining adventure. It's like being a real-life superhero!

So, there you have it, high-budget explorers. Nashville is a city of luxury and elegance, with experiences that will make you feel like a star. Whether you're enjoying top-notch music, fine dining, or luxurious accommodations, Music City is ready to show you the finer side of life.

Whether you're traveling with pockets full or pockets light, this city welcomes you with open arms and a symphony of adventures.

For those on a budget, there's a world of free and low-cost wonders waiting to be explored. From free concerts to outdoor adventures, Nashville offers a plethora of thrifty treasures that won't break the bank. So, pack your sense of adventure and hit the town!

With a medium budget, you can dive into a world of science, history, art, and more. Nashville's moderate-budget marvels provide you with a range of experiences, from the depths of music history to the heights of creativity.

And if you're ready to really splurge, Nashville on a high-budget offers a taste of luxury. From backstage tours at legendary music venues to fine dining and pampering at elegant hotels, step into the lap of opulence.

No matter your budget, Nashville's diverse neighborhoods, rich music scene, delectable cuisine, and beautiful seasons are there for you to explore. So let's hit the town whatever your budget, after all, in Nashville, the only limit to your adventure is your imagination.

10

The Ultimate Family Adventure

Wow, can you believe all the amazing stuff we've done in Nashville? This city I call home, is full of music, history, art, yummy food, neighborhoods, and family adventures. We've danced to awesome tunes, traveled back in time, seen colorful art, and tried the tastiest food ever. We've explored the coolest neighborhoods, and guess what? There's something fun for everyone, whether you have a little money or a lot.

From the Grand Ole Opry to the streets of East Nashville, our adventure has been a blast. We've learned about country music, discovered hidden gems, and found out about famous places. We've eaten hot chicken, barbecue, and southern comfort food, and we've tasted food from all around the world.

Nashville's neighborhoods are like characters in a story. East Nashville is artsy, South Nashville is full of culture, West Nashville has cool shops, North Nashville is all about community, and downtown Nashville is where the music is loudest.

It doesn't matter how much money you have; Nashville has fun stuff for all budgets. We've found free and cheap things to do, and we've checked out the fancier stuff, too.

But guess what? Our adventure doesn't have to stop here. Nashville is always changing, with new restaurants, art, and music. So, keep exploring and discovering new things.

And, here's a secret: you can help other families by leaving a review on Amazon. Your words can inspire them to have their very own Nashville adventure.

So, thanks for joining me on this journey through Nashville. And like we like to say here 'y'all come back now, ya hear?'

11

Bonus Itinerary

If I was crafting an itinerary for three epic days in Nashville, here's what I would do:

DAY 1:

Breakfast: We'd start our adventure with a visit to "Stay Golden." They make the most awesome biscuits in all of Tennessee. It's like having a cloud for breakfast. Don't leave without having their secret recipe Chocolate Chip Cookie, their the best.

Morning Activity: Next, we'd head to "Lane 5 Woodworks." They create amazing wooden things, and it's like exploring a magical forest of furniture. Plus, they sometimes show how to make cool wood stuff.

Lunch: For lunch, we'd dig into some hot chicken at "Hattie B's." It's super spicy and delicious! You might even feel like a fire-breathing dragon, but it's so worth it.

Afternoon Activity: In the afternoon, we'd go to the "Adventure Park at Nashville." There are ziplines, rope courses, and even treehouses! It's like being in a jungle.

Dinner: For dinner, we'd munch on some finger-licking good BBQ at "Peg Legs BBQ." They've got the yummiest ribs and pulled pork sandwiches.

Evening Activity: And in the evening, we'd head to "The Gallery of Iconic Guitars" (GIG) at Belmont University. Check out the awesome guitars played by famous musicians and then stroll around the University campus.

DAY 2:

Breakfast: We'd kick off day two with breakfast at a local bakery called "Sunflower Bakehouse." They make the fluffiest pastries and tastiest muffins.

Morning Activity: Soundwaves Waterpark: start your morning off on the lazy river and then pick up some speed on the slides.

Lunch: For lunch, we'd grab some yummy barbecue at "Mission Barbecue." Their pulled pork sandwiches are so good and make sure to try the cornbread. It's worth jumping out of the water for this delicious barbeque baby.

Afternoon Activity: After lunch, we'd spend more time at "Sound-Waves." Hang out by the wave pool and watch some music videos and then grab a tub for some fun on the outdoor slides.

BONUS ITINERARY

Dinner: Dinner would be at "Bavarian Bierhaus" They serve authentic German food and it's close to Soundwaves.

Evening Activity: To end the day, we'd go to "The Nashville Palace." It's a place for live music and dancing. You can two-step and have fun like a real cowboy or cowgirl.

DAY 3:

Breakfast: On day three, we'd start with a big breakfast at "Pancake Pantry." They make all kinds of pancakes, and they're super fluffy and tasty. Get there early so you don't have to wait in line too long.

Morning Activity: After breakfast, we'd go on a hunt for murals in East Nashville. It's like a colorful treasure hunt with art all over the streets. Then stop into Shelby Bottoms Park for a stroll by the river.

Lunch: For lunch, we'd visit "Pharmacy Burger & Beer Garden". You'll love the outdoor seating and the burgers are outstanding; make sure to get them with the tater tots.

Afternoon Activity: In the afternoon, we'd explore "Cheekwood Estate and Gardens." Take in the beautiful views of these wonderful gardens.

Dinner: Our last dinner would be at "The Smiling Elephant" They serve mouthwatering authentic Thai food.

Evening Activity: To end our adventure, we'd go to "The Listening Room." It's a fantastic live show. Be sure to try the fried pickles as a snack.

So if I was your personal tour guide, this is how I'd recommend spending three days in Nashville. But that's just me; now it's your turn to dream up your time in Nashville, TN. Have fun!

One last thing, don't forget to leave a review on Amazon after you've had the very best time in Nashville, TN thanks to this guide.

About the Author

Hi, I'm Josiah! I'm 10 years old and I live in Nashville, TN, I love my city. I love it when people visit and I get to show them Nashville's charm, all the main attractions and hidden gems. I wrote this book because I want to take you along on an adventure through Nashville, like you had me as your tour guide.